Your Educational Success

YES

Foundation

Workbook

Leticia Colon de Mejias

Mariposa Publishing

Contents

Introduction

"Every Journey Begins with the first step." ~ Author unknown

AT THE CORE OF GROWTH IS DEDICATION TO CHANGE

You may have begun reading this book because you have made a decision to dedicate yourself to your professional and educational growth. It may have been years or months since you were last in an educational setting. You may feel apprehensive about what will be required of you. You may be worried about not having the time to study, or wondering if you will do well.

For a moment set your concerns aside. Focus on your choice to be here because you desire to change and grow. Today you are starting out on a new journey. Learning is a life long process. Starting today your goals are to learn, grow, to seek new ideas, develop new understandings and apply your learned skills in your workplace and lives.

Educational success and professional growth go hand in hand, and are linked in many ways. Success and growth require focus and the abilities to create goals, organize thoughts, and manage time. Success and growth also require strong verbal and written communication skills, development of strong interpersonal skills and the ability to reflect on one's current situation.

Personal development grows from educational and professional success. To grow as an employee and as an individual you will utilize skills you may already have and develop new skills. The first step on any journey is to choose a direction. Our direction or course may change during our journey, but each of us must start somewhere.

OBJECTIVES

When you complete this module you will be able to:

- Utilize a goal-setting process
- Utilize lists and time management to accomplish goals
- Identify barriers to success and develop ways to overcome them
- Give and receive feedback in a positive and professional manner
- Be a successful part of an educational team
- Complete college enrollment forms
- Complete financial aid and tuition reimbursement forms
- Select classes that apply to your educational goals
- Research promotional opportunities
- Find help when you need support or have questions about your educational goals

Chapter 1

Today is your first step on the journey to Your Educational Success.

GOALS AND PLANNING

- **Setting goals**
- **Developing a plan**

Our personal goals and desires are continually evolving. As humans we continue to desire new things and better circumstances. Having desires and setting goals are not the same thing. Wanting something is familiar to all of us. Setting a goal is the first step in developing a plan to acquire the things we desire.

If you want to have a Bachelor's degree you can say, "I want a college degree." Most of us realize that we cannot expect to get the degree based on our desire alone. We must lay the foundations to go to college and finish a degree program. The goal of getting your college degree will consist of a plan with many small steps leading you to your larger goal.

REFLECT ON YOUR CURRENT GOALS

What are your current goals and desires?

_____

_____

_____

_____

_____

_____

_____

What are some steps you need to take to lay the foundation for these goals to come to realization? Keep in mind that listing your goals, and writing down the steps you will need to take to reach them, is the first step to building a plan that you can then follow to completion.

_____

_____

_____

_____

_____

_____

_____

_____

_____

_____

_____

_____

_____

_____

_____

_____

_____

_____

_____

_____

_____

_____

_____

_____

_____

_____

_____

_____

_____

EXERCISES

Learning about what's out there for you! How can you find out what options are available for you to increase your educational experience and polish your job skills? How can you begin to set goals that will support your professional growth and development?

This week you will begin thinking about the type of careers you might enjoy.

Journal Exercise 1: List all the careers you have an interest in.

Example list: teacher, doctor, physical therapist, radiation technologist.

_____

_____

_____

_____

_____

_____

_____

_____

_____

_____

_____

_____

_____

_____

Journal Exercise 2: Break down each career you listed in Exercise 1.

Under each career you listed write your thoughts and feelings about each role, and then list any information you have gathered about each role. Write freely; go on-line to look up roles, educational requirements or training costs.

Example: Teacher - Works with children or adult learners, requires a 4 year degree, two years can be done at a community college level, must attend a 4 year college for BA program, must pass teacher certification test, makes about $35,000 starting salary, $60,000 and up with a master's degree, must apply to college, finish college, pass test, like people, be organized.

_____

_____

_____

_____

_____

_____

_____

_____

_____

_____

_____

_____

_____

_____

_____

_____

_____

_____

Chapter 2

"I am willing to put myself through anything; temporary pain or discomfort means nothing to me as long as I can see that the experience will take me to a new level. I am interested in the unknown, and the only path to the unknown is through breaking barriers." ~ Diana Nyad

IDENTIFYING BARRIERS TO SUCCESS

- **What options will best suit your current life situation?**
- **Possible barriers to goals**
- **Brainstorming about ways to overcome barriers**

We have all encountered barriers in our lives. What makes the difference between overcoming or being held back by barriers? There are many theories as to why one person succeeds while another fails. People who can effectively identify barriers have better success in overcoming them. Being able to identify the source of a problem (or barrier) is the first step in solving the problem. "First find the problem, then you can begin to fix it." Once you have identified barriers or possible barriers, you can then begin to look at ways to avoid them.

Step 1: Looking for barriers or problems that can impede your goal.

Step 2: Brainstorming ways to avoid or overcome the barriers.

Looking ahead

Taking the time to plan will support choices that can assist your overall personal and professional growth. Troubleshooting is an essential part of planning. Looking ahead and thinking about possible problems with a plan can be used in any environment. This exercise can apply to home, school, or work.

Below is an example of troubleshooting before starting something new.

Sheryl was about to begin a new job. She had hired a baby sitter and was given a new car by her family. Before her first day of work she had the sitter come over and meet her child to be sure the care situation would work out. She had her car tuned up and put gas in the car. She drove to her new job and located parking. She timed the trip to see how long the drive would take in morning traffic. She even looked at the bus schedule. In case her car ever had a problem, she could take the bus to work. She spoke with her aunt and arranged a back up care plan if her child became ill.

Is there anything else Sheryl could have done to prepare for her new job? Take the time to discuss this as a group.

_____

_____

_____

_____

_____

_____

_____

_____

_____

_____

_____

Why is identifying barriers an important step to reaching a goal?

_____

_____

_____

_____

_____

_____

_____

_____

_____

_____

_____

_____

_____

_____

_____

_____

_____

_____

_____

EXERCISES

Journal Exercise 3: List any current barriers to your educational or work-related goals.

Example: Lack of childcare, lack of time, unorganized, lack of money, confused about what to study, worried about starting/returning to school, fear of failing.

_____

_____

_____

_____

_____

_____

_____

Journal Exercise 4: List all the positive things about yourself that will support your goals. Brainstorm about ideas that can help you reach your goals.

Example: Fast learner, determined, desire to finish school, supportive family or supervisor, flexible schedule, tuition reimbursement program at work.

_____

_____

_____

_____

_____

_____

_____

_____

_____

_____

_____

_____

_____

Journal Exercise 5: Making good choices. List any potential barriers and changes you can make to support your new goals?

Example: Problem - Lack of Funds.

Solution 1: Start a savings account and direct deposit $25.00 a week.

Solution 2: Look into financial aid programs at the colleges.

Solution 3: Look into tuition reimbursement programs at your job.

_____

_____

_____

_____

_____

_____

_____

_____

_____

_____

_____

_____

Chapter 3

"Tell me and I'll forget; show me and I may remember; involve me and I'll understand."
~ *Chinese Proverb*

WE ALL LEARN DIFFERENTLY

Some people learn best by listening. Learning by listening is called audio learning. Others learn best by doing. Hands-on learning is called tactile learning. Many learn best by watching someone do something. This is called visual learning. Most people learn best with a mixed approach or combination of these styles.

Knowing how you learn best can help you to decide what type of learning path you should take. Ask yourself questions like:
- Do I enjoy reading alone?
- Do I understand what I read easily?
- Am I motivated to pick up a book and learn a new skill by reading?
- Do I enjoy listening to someone explain a new skill or subject?
- Do I retain what I hear?
- Do I learn best by doing something and learning while I attempt to complete a task?
- Do I enjoy listening to books on CD or on tape?
- Do I need to take frequent breaks and move around?

Depending on your answers, you can then begin to think about what types of programs would be best for you. If you are self-motivated and understand a subject by reading about it, you may do well with on-line classes. If you need frequent breaks, on-line classes offer you the chance to move around and go back to your studying later. However, if you prefer to hear about a subject and discuss it with peers you may not enjoy on-line learning.

How can you become a successful learner?
- Know how you learn best.
- Use your positive qualities to develop a personalized study plan.
- Locate and use existing supports. This would include things like study groups, on-line tutoring web sites, friends and family.
- Create new supports. Start a study group with your classmates.
- Set aside time to study weekly
- Practice patience and diligence in your study plan.
- Establish a comfortable place to study.
- Establish a study schedule and stick to it.
- Don't over book your time or overwhelm yourself.

Use textbook cues
Textbook cues direct you to important areas in the text. Here are some cues to watch for:
- Bold font type
- Italicized font type
- Underlining
- Boxes
- Diagrams
- Key definitions
- Chapter reviews

Avoid distraction
Self-sabotage is often a primary cause of failure. Avoiding interruptions requires planning and troubleshooting.

How many times have you sat down to read or write at home and suddenly the dust bunnies under the couch seem to be calling to you: "Stop working and come dust under here." Isn't it funny how the dust bunnies did not bother us until we attempted to focus on something? This is our attempt to avoid working on our goal. Shifting our focus to tasks like cleaning or laundry during study time is often our way of avoiding something we are not sure we can accomplish.

Putting first things first

Prioritizing is not just something we do at work. We also need to prioritize things we need to get done on our personal time. We must keep our goals in mind and stay the course. If it is study time then we must not fall prey to distractions.

Tips (planning ahead for study time)

- Find a quiet place to study.
- Get ample sleep daily. Study when you are rested
- Eat balanced meals. Have snacks with you when you study.
- Use music if it helps you focus or block out background noise.
- Reward positive progress. For example, set small goals, i.e., I will study for an hour and then take a thirty-minute break if I do well.
- Try studying with a friend. Try to choose a friend who will stay focused.
- Be honest with yourself about how long studying will take, and then plan the time you will need to complete the task.
- Avoid "cramming" or trying to study everything in a short time frame. Instead plan to study and complete assignments in increments. You won't feel overwhelmed if you break large assignments into smaller pieces of work.

EXERCISES

Journal Exercise 6: What type of learner do you think you are?

_____

_____

_____

_____

_____

_____

_____

_____

Journal Exercise 7: Identify two study supports for your learning style.

_____

_____

_____

_____

_____

_____

_____

_____

Chapter 4

"Man's mind, once stretched by a new idea, never regains its original dimensions."
~ Oliver Wendell Holmes

LEARN AND SHARE WHAT YOU LEARN

Learning is the act, process, or experience of gaining knowledge or skills. Learning enhances our abilities.

In order for us to fully participate in the process, we should:

1. Be actively involved in the experience;
2. Make a commitment to learn what is being taught;
3. Ask questions about anything you are not clear on;
4. Develop and share your own thoughts; and
5. Pledge to apply the new knowledge in your life and in the lives of others.

Let's explore viewing a movie and using the movie content to create talking points. We will examine our current skill sets and those needed to share our ideas with the class.

When you read something or watch something on television do you critique the content or explore the purpose of the book or show?

As a group we will view a video and develop the following ideas:

- What was the filmmaker's purpose in creating the film?
- Did the filmmaker support his or her ideas with facts?
- Was the film successful in swaying your personal beliefs?
- Did it challenge what you knew about the subject prior to seeing the film?

EXERCISES

Watch the provided DVD and write a five paragraph paper about the film. Answer the following questions:

1. What was the message the filmmakers were trying to get across?
2. What did you learn from watching the film?
3. Will watching the film change the way you behave or things you do?

Write a sentence that summarizes the film's main idea. Develop the sentence into a full paragraph about the film's content.

Journal Exercise 8: (Group discussion question) - Why is it important to focus on finding the purpose of what we read or view?

_____

_____

_____

_____

_____

_____

_____

_____

_____

Chapter 5

"Better three hours too soon, than a minute too late." ~ William Shakespeare

TIME MANAGEMENT

- **To-Do lists**
- **How to make a list that you can follow**
- **To-Do list vs. a Calendar**

What do you put on a To-Do list?
- To-Do lists should list items that you must get done.
- To-Do lists do not include appointments.
- Appointments should be listed on your calendar.

A good way to determine what should go on your To-Do list is to ask yourself "does this task need to be done on a specific day?" If the answer is yes, then you should put the item on your calendar. The item should be listed on the date it must be done by. If the item is a task that needs to be done, but is not based on a specific time line, you can place it on a To-Do list. Some items might be placed on both a To-Do list and a calendar.

EXAMPLES

TASK	TO-DO LIST	CALENDAR	COMMENTS
Complete college application	✓	✓	Calendar: Put on the actual due date.
Child's doctor's appointment		✓	
Work schedule		✓	
Laundry	✓		
Get oil changed in car	✓		
Look at college web sites	✓		
Complete financial aid forms	✓	✓	Calendar: Put on the actual due date.
Research paper due	✓	✓	Calendar: List items such as research for paper, draft paper, final paper due. Put on the actual due date for each phase of the paper.

EXERCISES

"Ordinary people think merely of spending time. Great people think of using it."
~Author Unknown

Journal Exercise 9: On your calendar or date book, list your work schedule and all classes you are enrolled in. List any weekly or monthly recurring appointments. Be sure to include appointments that are for family members if you provide transportation or care. Use the space below to brainstorm possible calendar listings.

_____

_____

_____

_____

_____

_____

_____

_____

_____

_____

Journal Exercise 10: Create a To-Do list of important items required to start college next semester.

_____

_____

_____

_____

_____

Chapter 6

"Dost thou love life? Then do not squander time, for that is the stuff life is made of."
~ Benjamin Franklin

TIME AND THE WAY THE WORLD WORKS

- **Time lines**
- **Calendars**
- **A college year / Selecting courses**
- **Meeting with a college adviser**

Colleges run on schedules. These schedules are important to your educational success. To get into and complete a degree or certificate program, you must plan your time around when you need to:

- Complete financial aid paperwork and forms
- Enroll in classes
- Attend classes
- Study and complete homework

You will also need to consider your personal life and other commitments you already have. As adult learners we have many responsibilities we did not have when we were younger. We work, care for our homes, and care for our families. We may volunteer or have other commitments outside the workplace or home. We must always keep these commitments in mind. The best way to ensure we are able to keep these commitments and not get overwhelmed is to use a calendar and To-Do lists. We must set time aside to meet our goals and follow through on our long-term plans.

Many important goals are dictated by set time lines. Our jobs, colleges, and certificate programs run on set time lines. To be successful we must learn these time lines and work around them.

LEARNING HOW TO UTILIZE COLLEGE ADVISERS

To finish a degree program you must complete a preset group of classes. Each major has different requirements and it is important that you choose courses that will support you obtaining a degree or certification. Some required classes in your degree program may be offered only at certain times of the year. It is very frustrating to realize that you are missing required classes for a program.

To avoid any confusion it is best to schedule time to meet with a school adviser and plan your study program. A school adviser's job is to explain the degree requirements, required courses, schedules, and time lines. School advisers may make recommendations regarding planning and working around other responsibilities and commitments you may have.

It is important that you schedule recurring appointments with a school adviser. Often our responsibilities or commitments may change and therefore affect our ability to continue down a certain path. In some cases, the offered courses or times may change. In either case, you will need to re-evaluate and create a new plan of action. It is important that you always keep your goals in focus when attempting to balance completing a degree program and your other commitments.

EXERCISES

Journal Exercise 11: Go on-line and locate a college you are interested in.
Look up the colleges application deadline and enrollment deadlines.
Take notes on when you would apply for financial aid, register for classes, add or drop
classes, and how to contact your school adviser.

_____

_____

_____

_____

_____

_____

_____

_____

_____

_____

_____

_____

_____

_____

_____

_____

_____

Journal Exercise 12: Research a few college degree or certificate programs you are interested in. Prepare to meet with your adviser by reading about the degree programs and course requirements. Print or write down the information. Make an appointment to visit the college and meet with an adviser at the college of your choice. Make notes and bring them with you. Take notes while you talk with the adviser. Ask questions about any on-campus student support programs or free tutors.

_____

_____

_____

_____

_____

_____

_____

_____

_____

_____

_____

_____

_____

_____

_____

_____

_____

_____

YES Foundation Workbook

Chapter 7

"Shoot for the moon. Even if you miss, you'll land among the stars."
~ Brian Littrell

SECRETS OF MOTIVATED PEOPLE

When you make a plan, anticipate problems

"Before even trying to achieve a goal, target potential pitfalls and troubleshoot them." Peter Gollwitzer, a professor of psychology at New York University, says that "people who plan for obstacles are more likely to stick with projects than those who don't." Real-life has real problems. Before you start working on something, try to identify potential problems, and then find ways to avoid them.

Authors often use this strategy when writing a book. For example, they install blinds on home-office doors to minimize disruptions. They also establish rules, like checking e-mail only after they have written for two hours. It is easier to follow a plan than to wrestle with every distraction at the moment.

Keep a positive attitude. *I think I can, I think I can...YES I CAN...*

"A person's success is often based on what she believes about her abilities, not on how objectively talented she is", according to research by Albert Bandura, a professor of psychology at Stanford University. Bandura's work has shown that people who believe they can succeed have a better chance of accomplishing what they set out to do.

Don't set unrealistic goals

When your sights are too ambitious, they can burn you out by overwhelming you. Instead of aiming unrealistically high, set goals that are a stretch but not an overreach. For example, come up with a doable savings plan for your budget, look at financial aid and tuition reimbursement plans, plan your courses around the budget.

Set small steps toward reaching your larger goal. For example, if your goal is to get a college degree in four years, then set a goal about how many credits or classes you will take each year.

Write both your small and large goals in a place you will see them everyday. Looking at your goals keeps them fresh in your mind and helps you stay focused. Remember that you can't reach large goals overnight, so it is important to set small goals that you can reach and feel good about. Each small step will bring you closer to your larger goal.

Go public with it

Talk about your new goals with friends and family. Talking to people close to you about what you are working on starts your goals in motion. First, the people around you will understand you are changing because it is important to you. Second, your friends and family will understand that you may need their help and support. For example, your family may offer to help with childcare so you can return to college, or may help cook a meal one night a week to allow you time to study. Once you start talking about your plans, people may reach out to support you. After you start taking steps toward your goals, things often fall into place on their own.

Identify supports before you start out and use them when you are struggling

Before starting on your goal, think of friends and family who truly want to see you succeed. Talking with people close to you before you start out on a new path allows them the time they may need to prepare mentally for the changes that will come. Then, when you need support the people around you will be ready to help you. Don't be afraid to ask for support.

Make yourself a priority

Put your needs first, even when it feels selfish. You will derail your progress if you sacrifice yourself for others in order to please them. Keep your long-term goals in mind when you are making daily choices. Don't participate in things that do not support your long-term plans.

Challenge yourself and change your routine

It's hard to remain enthusiastic when everything stays the same. Changing your study routine when you are having trouble can help keep you focused. Try going to the library or studying with a friend. Try using music to motivate you, or take a quick walk before you study for a change of pace.

Keep on learning

Enjoy the process of getting to the goal, rather than just eyeing the finish line. When you are looking for jobs try volunteering in the area of your interest. This can often lead to new skills learned and new doors opened.

Remember the deeper meaning

You're more likely to realize a goal when it has true personal significance to you. Write your goals down and the deeper underlying reason you desire to reach these goals. Looking at this when you doubt yourself is a great way to stay on track. For example, working full time and going to college may mean spending less time with family and friends. Reminding yourself that a college degree can lead to promotions, new opportunities and better pay can help you stay focused.

Dealing with setbacks

We all have had setbacks at one point or another. What sets people apart is not what setbacks they face, but how they react to them. Whatever the problem or obstacle, it will eventually come to pass. It is important to keep the bigger picture in mind; remember that greater things lay ahead.

How you react to a setback will determine how successful you will be. Always keep a positive attitude. Take a moment to evaluate the situation; be objective. Take responsibility for your mistakes, but do not dwell on them.

Plan your next steps while keeping in mind your goals. Do not be afraid to ask for help. People are more often than not willing to support you. It is not uncommon for people to believe that they are the only ones dealing with a problem. You may be surprised by how many people may have experienced a similar situation.

Re-evaluate your plan. If needed, start the plan over. Be realistic. Set achievable steps. Be flexible and allow room for other setbacks. Above all, keep moving forward.

Setbacks are a part of the process, but it is ultimately up to you to choose whether or not you will be successful. Keep reaching for your goals.

EXERCISES

Journal Exercise 13: How can you apply these strategies to your goals?

_____

_____

_____

_____

_____

_____

_____

_____

_____

_____

_____

_____

_____

_____

_____

_____

Chapter 8

"It is a melancholy truth that even great men have their poor relations."
~ Charles Dickens

PEOPLE SKILLS

- **How to work well with others**
- **How to deal with difficult people**
- **Motivating others to work as a team**

Working well with others

Never criticize others

- People don't see their own faults, no matter how wrong they may be. Your criticism will not be helpful. Criticism can hurt others and ruin relationships. Criticism puts others on the defensive, hurts self-esteem and builds resentment.
- People respond to positive behavior. Be genuinely interested in other people.
- People are most interested in themselves. If you share that interest, they will respond. If you talk to people about themselves, they will keep listening and listening.
- Remember people's names and other important personal details about them.

Be a good listener

- Urge others to talk about themselves.
- Give them your exclusive attention.
- Listen to their concerns/complaints. You will ease tension and build relationships.
- Be eager to hear from those who may complain about you or people you represent, however wrong those complaints may be. Impress upon them how eager you are to hear them. Thank them for bringing up their concerns.

Make the other person feel important

- Use people's names whenever possible. People yearn to feel important and appreciated.
- Continually recognizing someone's expertise and capabilities will make them feel important. They will want to demonstrate their expertise by possibly helping you.
- Give others clear authority over a part of a larger project and help them understand their tangible contributions. They'll become more committed to the success of the project.
- Be sincere and avoid flattery.

Smile

- Greet others with enthusiasm and animation. A smile tells others that you like them and are glad to see them.
- Smile even when on the phone; the smile will be clear in the tone of your voice.
- Work as a team; Cooperate.

How to deal with difficult people

"If you argue, ridicule, and contradict, you may achieve a victory sometimes; but it will be an empty victory, because you will never get your opponent's good will."

~ *Ben Franklin*

You can't win an argument

- Most arguments end with each person more certain of his or her opinions and less willing to change them. Even if you win, you may hurt the pride of the other person and he or she will resent you for it.

Avoiding arguments

- Welcome disagreements.
- Stay calm.
- Listen first. Hear others out.
- Identify areas of agreement.
- Admit your errors to make it easier for others to admit theirs.
- If there is no resolution to be found, delay action and promise to consider their side further.

You catch more bees with honey

- Starting conversations with sincere praise, appreciation and empathy will help make the other person feel more open to what you have to say.
- Beginning with a friendly tone will help the others to be more open minded.

Allow others to give their side

- Allow others to finish talking. Don't interrupt. Others won't pay attention to you until they've had their own say.

Empathize with the other person's ideas and desires

- People want others to be sympathetic to their problems. Empathize as much as you can. Try something like "I understand you are upset, but take a step back and look at the bigger picture." "Is there anything I can do for you?"

Respect the opinion of others

- Never say "you're wrong." People don't like to admit even to themselves that may be wrong.
- Body language can also communicate "you're wrong."
- Don't immediately assume you're right. Demonstrating your willingness to rationally examine the facts will inspire others to do likewise.

If you are wrong, admit it quickly and dramatically

- Admitting your errors clears guilt and frees everyone to move toward solutions more quickly. People will respect you more for your honesty when you can admit your own faults.

Try to see things from the other person's point of view

"If there is any one secret to success, it lies in the ability to get the other person's point of view and see things from that person's angle as well as your own." ~ Henry Ford

- Understanding another's point of view is the key to understanding their decisions. Seeing their point of view is key to motivating them.
- Frame requests in terms of what others find motivating.

Motivating others to work as a team

Begin with positive comments and honest appreciation
- It is easier to take criticism after we've heard some praise.
- Look for positive talking points before calling attention to failings.
- Follow up sincere praise with an "and" rather than a "but" before delivering criticism. Otherwise, your praise may seem contrived and artificial.

Talk about your own mistakes before criticizing the other person
- Criticism is easier to bear when you share your own mistakes. Others will be more motivated to correct themselves. Explain a time when you may not have done your best, or when you made a mistake.

Call attention to people's mistakes indirectly
- Asking the other party to consider alternative points of view, i.e. "Is this process the most efficient way to get the job done?" And "I wonder how user-friendly this feature will be."
- Rather than pointing out a sales clerk's inattentiveness toward customers, a store manager might help out the customer in full view of the inattentive sales clerk.
- Instead of "Your idea isn't very good," try "This idea may not work in the present environment." Don't be too obvious.

Let the other person save face.
- Give others a chance to avoid embarrassment. Damaging someone's ego will build resentment in the long run.
- Always try to give criticism in private. Don't make the individual look bad in front of his/her peers. "Praise in public, criticize in private."

- Ask the person if they could have handled the situation differently. Often, the person realizes they did not necessarily do their best.

Make the fault seem easy to correct. Use encouragement.
- You can enable others to succeed by making faults seem easy to correct and new skills seem easy to learn.

Praise the slightest improvement and praise every improvement

"Abilities wither under criticism; they blossom under encouragement." ~ Dale Carnegie

- Praise will reinforce the growth of desired behavior – and bad habits "will shrink due to lack of attention."
- Try to be as specific as possible - it should come from the heart and be completely sincere.

Give the other person a fine reputation to live up to
- For example, "You have been such a capable producer in the past, but your recent projects haven't been up to your old standards."

EXERCISES

Journal Exercise 14: Journal about a time that you argued with a friend or co-worker. Write about what happened and the result of the argument. Write about ways the argument could have been resolved or avoided. Remember to use complete sentences and proofread your work.

_____

_____

_____

_____

_____

_____

_____

_____

_____

_____

_____

_____

_____

_____

_____

_____

_____

_____

Journal Exercise 15: Talk with your peers about your reactions to this chapter's material. List your thoughts and discussion points.

_____

_____

_____

_____

_____

_____

_____

_____

_____

_____

_____

_____

_____

_____

_____

_____

_____

_____

_____

_____

_____

_____

_____

Journal Exercise 16: Write about a time you witnessed a problem at work that could have been avoided by using one of the ideas in this Chapter. Note the concern and how it could have been handled differently.

_____

_____

_____

_____

_____

_____

_____

_____

_____

_____

_____

_____

_____

_____

_____

_____

_____

_____

_____

Chapter 9

"Words like birds once released cannot be caged again." ~ unknown

THE WRITTEN WORD

The ability to express an idea in writing is an essential skill. This skill takes practice. But practice does not make perfect; practice makes permanent. Practice is useful if we practice the correct way to do something. To write well we must have a good understanding of the parts in a sentence. Look up the following words and list their definitions for reference.

Grammar Definitions

Use the following Link to look up the definitions of the words:
http://grammar.ccc.commnet.edu/grammar/

Noun:

_____

_____

_____

Pronoun:

_____

_____

_____

Verb:

_____

_____

_____

Adjective:

_____

_____

_____

Adverb:

_____

_____

_____

Prepositional phrase:

_____

_____

_____

_____

EXERCISES

Journal Exercise 17: List 10 examples of each type of word you defined on the previous page.

_____

_____

_____

_____

_____

_____

_____

_____

_____

_____

_____

_____

_____

_____

_____

_____

_____

_____

Chapter 10

MAKING SENSE OF SENTENCES

Sentence: Expresses a complete thought, has a subject (noun), shows action (verb) and has proper punctuation and grammar.

To make a sentence you need three things:

1. A sentence is a group of words used together that makes sense on its own.

   "Cheese, car, house, table on Tuesday." - Nonsense. This isn't a sentence - it doesn't make sense.

   "I parked my car next to my house." - Sentence. You can understand what it means. It makes sense on its own.

2. Good writing requires correct punctuation and grammar. Correct punctuation allows the reader to understand your writing.
   - A sentence must begin with a capital letter.
   - A sentence must end with a full-stop (.), a question mark (?) or an exclamation mark (!).

   NOTE! Sometimes people confuse the punctuation to use at the end of a sentence. You can use commas (,) colons (:) or semicolons (;) in your writing, but they should never be used instead of a full-stop.

3. A complete sentence also needs a subject and a predicate. The subject is usually a noun or pronoun and the predicate is a verb (a doing or being word.)

SUBJECT - noun or pronoun. This is the person, or thing, that is doing the verb.

Example of nouns: Jane, Tuesday, dog, table, and Boston.

Example of pronouns: I, we, you, who, he, she, it, they, this, these, that, those, and somebody.

VERB (a doing or being word) - predicate.
Example of verbs: is, cooking, walked, need, was, and am.

Here are some examples of sentences. Circle the verbs and underline the subjects:

1. Last week Peggy redecorated the pub.

2. Are you hungry yet?

3. Martin, be quiet.

4. Tuesday was very rainy and cold.

Other things to know about sentences

Sentences can be short or long. There is no limit on the number of words you may use in a sentence. It all depends on you and the effect you want the sentence to have. The important thing is to always keep the reader in mind.

Sentences that run on too long are like boring speeches. The reader may fall asleep. If your sentences go on too long, it may be a good idea to break them up. Look to see if you have mistakenly created run-on sentences.

It is also important to remember that you don't always need to write in sentences. For example, a shopping list doesn't need sentences, but a job application or an e-mail does.

Online Links: View the following links this week.

http://grammar.ccc.commnet.edu/grammar/ppt/fragments.pps

http://grammar.ccc.commnet.edu/grammar/ppt/run-ons.pps

EXERCISES

Journal Exercise 18: Write 10 sentences.

_____

_____

_____

_____

_____

_____

_____

_____

_____

_____

_____

_____

_____

_____

_____

Journal Exercise 19: Circle the noun or pronouns in each sentence above, and underline the verb or verbs.

Journal Exercise 20: Go on-line and look up examples of college level entrance exam sentence questions.

_____

_____

_____

_____

_____

_____

_____

_____

_____

_____

_____

_____

_____

_____

_____

_____

_____

_____

_____

_____

Chapter 11

COMMAS AND TOPIC SENTENCES

Commas: When do I use a comma?

Commas are used for clarity when you have two complete ideas or thoughts in a sentence.

I am going to New York next week, and I will be going by bus. Notice the comma comes before the word "and", which is known as a conjunction or connector.

A conjunction is a word that is used as a connector. Other connectors you may use in your sentences are so, but, yet, for and nor.

Commas are also used when listing items. For example, John was to bring the ham, turkey, bread and mayo for the luncheon.

Online Links: View the following links this week.
http://grammar.ccc.commnet.edu/grammar/ppt/commas.pps#262,7,The English House of Commas

Topic Sentences: Topic + Controlling Idea

Before writing any essay or even a paragraph, it is important to think about the topic, and what you want to say about the topic. What you want to say about the topic is the controlling idea. Topic sentences should always contain both (1) a topic and (2) a controlling idea. When your introduction contains a clearly stated topic sentence, your reader will know what to expect and will understand your ideas.

Read the following topic sentences. They all contain a topic and a controlling idea.

1. People can avoid burglaries by taking certain precautions. (The precautions for...)
2. There are several advantages to growing up in a small town. (The advantages of...)
3. Most U.S. universities require a 550 point TOEFL score for a number of reasons. (The reasons for...)
4. Air pollution in Mexico City is the worst in the world for a number of reasons. (The causes of...) or (The effects of...)
5. Fixing a flat tire on a bicycle is easy if you follow these steps. (The steps for...)
6. There are several enjoyable ways to travel between the U.S. and Queretaro. (The ways to...) or (The methods of...)
7. Effective leadership requires specific qualities that anyone can develop. (The qualities (or characteristics or traits) of...)

A carefully thought out topic sentence will serve two important functions. First, it will provide you, the author, the means to stay focused on your objective. It's a lot easier to write if you know what you are going to write about! Second, a clearly stated topic sentence will provide readers with the tools they need to clearly understand what you have to say. These are important reasons to carefully consider topic sentences before you begin to write.

EXERCISES

Journal Exercise 21: Write 10 topic sentences. Remember to keep them open enough to allow you to write about the topic, but broad enough to keep your writing focused on one topic.

Chapter 12

WRITING, MAIN IDEAS, CONCLUSIONS, INTRODUCTIONS

- Why use a rough draft?
- Why is self-editing important?
- Why should you develop an outline?

Have you ever read a policy at work and wondered why it was written? What about looking for information on a website, but not being able to find what you are looking for?

Writing with your purpose in mind is important to ensure your reader can follow your train of thought. To develop your purpose you will need to create a rough draft. In your rough draft you develop your outline or train of thought.

Creating a rough draft
- Brainstorming
- Thesis statement
- Developing ideas
- Creating an outline

Brainstorming

Brainstorming means to generate ideas and write down all the ideas that come into your mind. You might want to focus on a question or a simple idea. Then you will list anything and everything that comes into your mind. At this stage no idea is a bad idea. Just write all your ideas down. Don't be critical of the ideas. Later you can scale your ideas back if needed.

Thesis statement

Developing and selecting a thesis statement is crucial to writing a good paper. First think about what you want to write about. Brainstorm and write your ideas down. The main idea of the paper should be stated in a sentence or two. The main idea reflects your stance on the subject.

For example, if we were writing about healthcare reform, and I thought the reform was important and should be supported, my thesis statement would be "Healthcare reform is crucial to the safety of all Americans." The thesis statement should be clear and specific to why it is important to reform healthcare. The thesis statement should also be written in a style that pulls the reader in. Use descriptive words the reader can relate to.

Developing your ideas

Developing your ideas requires you to think logically. Start at a high level and create an outline that you can expand on. Use each consecutive sentence to further support your idea. Continue to expand and break down each idea until you have clearly and accurately explained your stance before you move on.

- Write down the main points you want your reader to understand.
- Under each main point add supporting details.

Creating an outline

- Break the paper's main points into paragraphs. Each paragraph should follow a train of thought and contain a minimum of five to seven sentences. The sentences should support the paragraph's main idea.
- Develop your introduction.
- Develop the body of the paper.
- Develop your conclusion.

EXERCISES

Journal Exercise 22: Create a one-page paper.

1. Brainstorm ideas for a one-page paper.
2. Write a topic sentence.
3. Write a paragraph using your topic sentence.
4. Develop a paper outline.

_____

_____

_____

_____

_____

_____

_____

_____

_____

_____

_____

_____

_____

_____

_____

Chapter 13

HOW TO ANSWER QUESTIONS IN WRITING

- **Proper way to answer a question**
- **Spelling, using a dictionary and thesaurus**

There is a method to answering a question in writing. Whether you are writing for school, work or for personal reasons it is important to:

- Answer questions using complete sentences.
- Restate the question in your answer.
- Reread your answer to be sure you answered the question that was asked.
- Check your answer for spelling errors
- Check your answer for grammatical errors
- Be sure the answer makes sense and your reader can follow your train of thought.

Dictionaries and Online Search Engines

Spelling is important in any written document. Misspelled words confuse readers or make them miss your point entirely. Misspelled words lead the reader to believe that you did not take time to proofread, or that you are unprofessional. You can avoid misspellings by proofreading your documents and using spell-checkers to check your spelling. Most word processing applications have spelling programs that work automatically. When you handwrite a document or note it is important to use a dictionary or online search engine to find the correct spelling of a word. Be sure you check the word's meaning.

Words that sound the same

Many words sound the same but have different meanings. It is important to use the correct word to represent what you are trying to express.

The words to, too, and two are examples of words that sound the same but have different spelling and different meanings.

- **Two** is the number (I have two cats as pets.)
- **Too** can be used to mean excessive or in addition (there were too many kids at the party.)
- **To** means in the direction of (she went to the store.)

Another example of words that same but have different meanings are: there, their, they're.
- **Their** shows ownership (their mother is a teacher.)
- **They're** is a contraction for they are (they're going to the show.)
- **There** demonstrates a location (put the book over there on the shelf.)

Using an online search engine

There are many search engines you can use to look up words. If you add "definition" to the end of the word you are searching online, many of the search engine will return several online dictionaries and other reference materials you can use.

If you use one of the many word processor programs available today, you can look for dictionary and thesaurus tools on the "Tools" or "Language" menu drop down options. These options will provide definitions and alternative words you could use. These alternative words should help you understand word's meaning or its intended meaning.

Traditional dictionaries

When using a traditional dictionary you will find the word's spelling and meaning at the same time. The word may have more than one meaning, so be sure to read the meanings and select the best word. It is also a good idea to use a thesaurus when writing longer documents. Thesauruses can help broaden your vocabulary and add variety and spice to your writing or speaking. To use a dictionary you must know the first two letters of the word you are trying to spell. You will look for the letters in the top right and left corner of the pages. The pages are alphabetical. For example if you are looking to spell the word elevator. You would go to the "E" section of the dictionary, then look for the "El" section. Move down the page until you locate "Elev" words, then narrow your search until you find the needed spelling.

EXERCISES

Journal Exercise 23: List some commonly misused words below.

_____

_____

_____

_____

_____

_____

_____

_____

_____

_____

_____

_____

_____

Journal Exercise 24: List words you frequently misspell.

Look up and write down the correct spelling and meaning of these words.

_____

_____

_____

_____

_____

_____

_____

_____

_____

_____

_____

_____

_____

_____

_____

_____

_____

_____

_____

_____

_____

Journal Exercise 25: Practice answering the following questions in your class journal.
- What is brainstorming?
- Why is checking your spelling important?
- What are the four steps in creating a rough draft?
- Why is time management important?
- What does the statement, "you can't win an argument" mean to you?

_____

_____

_____

_____

_____

_____

_____

_____

_____

_____

_____

_____

_____

_____

_____

_____

_____

_____

Chapter 14

THE THREE C'S OF WRITING

Be clear. Be concise. Be concrete.

Clear

Does your writing makes sense? Can the reader follow your train of thought? Do you have a clear subject to focus on?

Before you begin to write, jot down your purpose and main message. Consider your audience when thinking of which words to use. If possible, relate your thought or ideas by using real-life examples. Real-life examples help bring your message home.

Concise

Have you removed excess wording and irrelevant ideas from your writing? The focus of your writing should be strictly on what you want your reader to understand.

It seems that everyone we know is busy. Keeping your writing to the point will keep your reader interested. People appreciate writers who stay focused. Getting and keeping people's attention is a real challenge. It is even harder to do when it's the written word. That's why it's critical to write with clarity.

Concrete

Have you cemented your words in your reader's mind? Is your writing supported with details and examples? Include stories or descriptions that help your reader visualize what you are trying to say. Your goal is to leave your reader with the feeling that you have an understanding about your subject matter. People love great stories. They can be extremely compelling and powerful. Take your audience on a journey with your words, story and message. Help your reader to hang onto your every word and image long after they have finished reading your work.

It is important in all writing to ensure you have followed the process below:

1. Mechanics - This refers to grammar. Look to see whether your essay has any grammatical mistakes.

2. Structure - This refers to the structure of your individual sentences. Look to see that you use a good variety of sentence structures and verbs. Verbs make your writing stronger and more interesting.

3. Organization - Is your entire essay well structured? Your essay should have a good introductory paragraph that contains a thesis statement, also known as the statement of purpose. You should finish the essay with a strong concluding paragraph. In addition, the paragraphs of your main body should be well-organized.

4. Development - You need to develop your ideas in your essay. This means that you need to give reasons and examples to support your viewpoints.

5. Focus - The message of your essay must be clear. Your essay must demonstrate a logical progression of thought and have a good flow. You should not discuss items that are only loosely related or unrelated to the essay topic.

EXERCISES

Journal Exercise 26: Watch a movie about food and answer the following question. What role do we play in our personal health?

_____

_____

_____

_____

_____

_____

_____

_____

_____

_____

_____

_____

_____

_____

_____

_____

_____

_____

Journal Exercise 27: Choose a topic for your research paper based in the subject matter of health and disease.

_____

_____

_____

_____

_____

_____

_____

_____

_____

_____

_____

_____

_____

_____

_____

_____

_____

_____

_____

Journal Exercise 28: Research your topic and create a rough draft for peer review.

_____

_____

_____

_____

_____

_____

_____

_____

_____

_____

_____

_____

_____

_____

_____

_____

_____

_____

_____

_____

_____

Chapter 15

CRITIQUING OTHER PEOPLE'S WORK

The ability to provide feedback to others is a valuable skill

We learned about providing feedback and how to work with our peers and co-workers. This week we will combine our people skills with our writing skills. Review your notes on both areas and use them to complete the exercises below.

Keep the following points in mind:

- **Honesty is important.** People need clear and honest feedback to improve their own skills and succeed. How you deliver the information will support how the person accepts it. Remember to keep in mind whom you are writing to, and how they may feel about what you say.

- **Be clear.** Give examples of areas the writer could improve. Note the paragraphs or page you are referring to and give suggestions not just criticism. Try phrases such as: You might want to try… This might be helpful… and then give an idea or two if needed. I was confused by… what did you mean by… This will allow the writer to respond and improve.

- **Keep the reader's feelings in mind.** Before you send your critique to the writer, re-read your work. Think about how you would feel reading the critique. Did you keep a positive tone? Did you talk about the good points as well as areas that could be improved? Did you give thorough feedback?

EXERCISES

Journal Exercise 29: Use the Three C's of writing to critique your peer's paper. On completion submit the critique to your peer and your coach.

_____

_____

_____

_____

_____

_____

_____

_____

_____

_____

_____

_____

_____

_____

_____

_____

_____

_____

Journal Exercise 30: Read your peer's critique and revise your paper for final submission.

_____

_____

_____

_____

_____

_____

_____

_____

_____

_____

_____

_____

_____

_____

_____

_____

_____

_____

_____

_____

Chapter 16

It is a mathematical fact that fifty percent of all doctors graduate in the bottom half of their class. ~ Author Unknown

SIMPLE FRACTIONS

- **What are fractions?**
- **Adding and Subtracting Fractions**
- **Multiplying Fractions**
- **Dividing Fractions**

What are fractions?

Fractions are numbers that represent parts of a whole. For example, if you cut a pie into eight slices, the eight slices make up the parts of the pie.

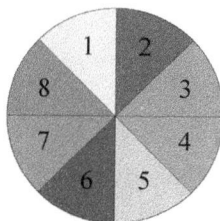

8 Slices = 1 Pie

Fractions are made up of two parts: *Numerator* and *Denominator*.

The *Numerator* is the top number and the *Denominator* is the bottom number.

Numerator: How many slices do you have?

$$\frac{8}{8} = 1 \text{ Pie}$$

Denominator: How many slices does it take to make up a whole pie?

If it takes eight slices to make up a pie and you have eight slices, then you have one whole pie.

Proper Fractions

The numerator or top of the fraction is smaller than the denominator or bottom of the fraction.

$$\frac{6}{8} \quad \textbf{Proper Fraction}$$

Improper Fractions

The numerator or top of the fraction is larger than the denominator or bottom of the fraction.

$$\frac{10}{8} \quad \textbf{Improper Fraction}$$

Mixed Number

A mixed number is the combination of a whole number and a fraction together.

$$1\frac{1}{2} \quad \textbf{Mixed Number}$$

Reducing

Reducing a fraction refers to reducing the fraction ratio to the lowest terms. A fraction is a ratio equal to the numerator/denominator. For example, the follow fractions are all equal because they can be reduced to the same fraction ratio:

$$\frac{50}{100} = \frac{25}{50} = \frac{5}{10} = \frac{1}{2}$$

In the example above, the lowest terms for the fraction ratio is $\frac{1}{2}$.

When finding the lowest terms for a fraction, it is important to remember that a fraction is a ratio. Therefore, what you do to the numerator, you must also do equally to the denominator. For example, if you start with the fraction **4/8** and divide the numerator and denominator by **4** each,

$$\frac{4 \; / \; 4 = 1}{8 \; / \; 4 = 2}$$

you end up with the fraction **1/2**, the lowest terms.

When you reduce a fraction to lowest terms, you find an equivalent fraction in which the numerator and denominator are as small as possible. This means that there is no number, except **1**, that can be divided evenly into both the numerator and the denominator.

One way of reducing fractions is to find the factors of the numerator and denominator. Factors are numbers that are only divisible by itself and 1, which when multiplied result in the desired number. For example, the fraction **10/50**, can be broken down into its factors.

$$\frac{10}{50} = \frac{2 \times 5}{5 \times 10} = \frac{2 \times 5}{5 \times 2 \times 5} = \frac{1}{5}$$

In this example, **10** can be broken down into the factors **2 x 5**, and **50** can be broken down into the factors **5 x 2 x 5**. When cross reduced the resulting fraction is **1/5**, which is its lowest terms.

Equivalent Fractions

Fractions that express the same ratio are equivalent (equal).

Equivalent fractions can be created by:
- reducing a fraction by dividing the numerator and denominator by the same number, or
- multiplying the numerator and denominator by the same number.

Adding and Subtracting Fractions

When adding, subtracting, or comparing fractions, it is useful to find the least common multiple of the denominators, often called the lowest common denominator.

To find the lowest common denominator, you first must find the common multiples of each denominator. Once you have found the common multiples, you then match them to find the lowest common multiple.

For example, if you wanted to add $\dfrac{1}{12} + \dfrac{5}{36}$, you would first find the common multiples for each denominator.

The common multiples for **12** are: **12, 24, 36, 48, 60, ...** (add 12 to each to get the next multiple).

The common multiples for **36** are: **36, 72, 108, 144, 180, ...** (add 36 to each to get the next multiple).

The smallest common number in both lists is the least common multiple, or the least common denominator. In this example, **36** is used because it is the least common multiple of both **12** and **36**.

Next you use the smallest common multiple to determine the new equivalent ratio. In this case **12 X 3 = 36**, so you would multiple both the top and bottom of the **1/12** fraction by **3**.

$$\frac{1 * 3 = 3}{12 * 3 = 36}$$

$$\frac{1}{12} + \frac{5}{36} = \frac{3}{36} + \frac{5}{36} = \frac{8}{36}$$

The sum of the two fractions can be reduced further by dividing the top and bottom by **4**.

$$\frac{8 \;/\; 4 = 2}{36 \;/\; 4 = 9}$$

REMEMBER: What you do to the numerator, you must do to the denominator.

Multiplying Fractions

Multiplying fractions consists of multiplying the numerators of both fractions together and multiplying the denominators of both fractions. The resulting fraction is a new ratio.

Four easy steps:
1. Reduce the individual fractions if you can
2. Cross reduce the simple fraction if you can
3. Multiply the numerator
4. Multiply the denominator
5. Reduce resulting fraction if you can

Cross Reducing

When you cross reduce you apply the same concept as when you reduce a simple fraction. The same rule applies; **What you do to the numerator, you must do to the denominator.**

For example, if you are multiplying **9/10** x **5/15**, see if you can reduce the individual fractions before you multiply them.

$$\frac{9}{10} \text{ x } \frac{5}{15} = \frac{9}{10} \text{ x } \frac{\cancel{5}^{1}}{\cancel{15}_{3}}$$

If you divide the numerator and denominator of the **5/15** fraction by **5**, you end up with **1/3**. Once you have reduced the individual fractions, write out the equation into a simple fraction.

$$\frac{9}{10} \text{ x } \frac{1}{3} = \frac{9 \text{ x } 1}{10 \text{ x } 3}$$

Next you check to see if you can cross reduce the numerator and denominator by the same number.

$$\frac{\overset{3}{\cancel{9}} \text{ x } 1}{10 \text{ x } \cancel{3}_{1}} = \frac{3 \text{ x } 1}{10 \text{ x } 1} = \frac{3}{10}$$

In the example above, if you divide the numerator and denominator by **3** you can cross reduce the **9** to **9/3 = 3**, and **3** to **3/3 = 1**. The resulting simple fraction cannot be cross reduced any further. Next you multiply the numerator and denominator across. The resulting fraction is equal to **3/10**. The last step is to check if you can further reduce the fraction. In this case, the resulting fraction cannot be reduced any further.

Dividing Fractions

Dividing fractions follows the same steps as multiplying fractions with the additional step of flipping the second fraction (the denominator will now be the numerator and vice versa.)

Five easy steps:
1. Reduce the individual fractions if you can
2. Flip the second fraction
3. Cross reduce the simple fraction if you can
4. Multiply the numerator
5. Multiply the denominators
6. Reduce resulting fraction if you can

For example, let's take a look at dividing $\frac{9}{10} \, / \, \frac{5}{15}$.

The first step would be to reduce the individual fractions if you can.

$$\frac{9}{10} \, / \, \frac{5}{15} = \frac{9}{10} \, / \, \frac{\cancel{5}^{\,1}}{\cancel{15}_{\,3}}$$

If you divide the numerator and denominator of the **5/15** fraction by **5**, you end up with **1/3**.

$$\frac{9}{10} \, / \, \frac{5}{15} = \frac{9}{10} \, / \, \frac{\cancel{5}^{\,1}}{\cancel{15}_{\,3}} = \frac{9}{10} \, / \, \frac{1}{3}$$

Once you have reduced the individual fractions to their lowest terms, flip the second fraction and write out the equation into a simple fraction.

$$\frac{9}{10} \, / \, \frac{1}{3} = \frac{9}{10} \, \text{x} \, \frac{3}{1} = \frac{9 \, \text{x} \, 3}{10 \, \text{x} \, 1}$$

Next you check to see if you can cross reduce the numerator and denominator by the same number. In the example above, the resulting simple fraction can not be cross reduced any further. Next you multiply the numerator and denominator across.

$$\frac{9 \, \text{x} \, 3}{10 \, \text{x} \, 1} = \frac{27}{10} = \frac{20}{10} + \frac{7}{10} = 2\frac{7}{10}$$

When you multiply the numerator and denominator across you get **27/10,** which is an improper fraction. Next you would check to see if you can reduce the resulting fraction. In this case, the fraction is at its lowest terms.

Finally, the improper fraction can be converted to a mixed number. Since **27 = 20 + 7,** you can rewrite the fraction **27/10 = 20/10 + 7/10 = 2 + 7/10 = 2 7/10.**

EXERCISES

Journal Exercise 31: Fractions

Visit the following web sites and work through the problems taking notes in your notebook.

Reducing fractions:

http://www.sosmath.com/algebra/fraction/frac3/frac33/frac33.html

Adding Fractions:

http://www.sosmath.com/algebra/fraction/frac3/frac37/frac37.html

Multiplying Fractions:

http://www.sosmath.com/algebra/fraction/frac3/frac34/frac34.html

Equivalent Fractions:

http://www.sosmath.com/algebra/fraction/frac3/frac36/frac36.html

Subtracting Fractions:

http://www.sosmath.com/algebra/fraction/frac3/frac38/frac38.html

Compound Fractions/ Mixed Numbers

http://www.sosmath.com/algebra/fraction/frac5/frac5.html

YES Foundation Workbook

Chapter 17

The essence of mathematics is not to make simple things complicated,
but to make complicated things simple. ~ S. Gudder

DECIMALS

- A decimal represents numbers less than a whole number.
- Decimals are written on the right side of the decimal point.
- Whole numbers are written on the left side of the decimal point.

NOTE: Think of the problem as a money problem: whole dollars are written on the left of the decimal, and cents are on written on the right of the decimal.

Decimals have places and each place represents fraction value.

For example;

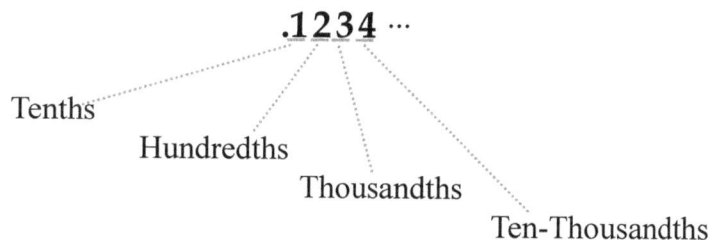

The number of decimal spaces to the right of the decimal point stretches out to infinity. In other words the decimal space values continue going; hundred-thousandths, millionths, ten-millionths, hundred-millionths, billionths, etc...

Adding and Subtracting Decimals

When adding or subtracting decimals, you should first align the decimal points vertically and add zeros as placeholders as needed.

Example: Adding 95 thousandths **(.095)** and 25 hundredths **(.25).**

Step 1: Align the decimal points vertically.

$$
\begin{array}{r}
.095 \\
+\ .25 \\
\hline
\end{array}
$$

Step 2: Add zeros as placeholders.

$$
\begin{array}{r}
.095 \\
+\ .250 \\
\hline
\end{array}
$$

Step 3: Add the columns farthest to the right first and work your way left. Remember to carry any values greater then 9 over to the next column on the left. In the thousandths column you add **5 + 0 = 5**. No values to carry over to the hundredths column.

$$
\begin{array}{r}
.095 \\
+\ .250 \\
\hline
5 \\
\end{array}
$$

Note: 25 hundredths is equal to 250 thousandths **(.25 = .250).**

In the hundredths column you add **9 + 5 = 14**. 14 hundredths = 1 tenths + 4 hundredths, so you carry over the 1 tenths.

$$
\begin{array}{r}
1 \\
.095 \\
+\ .250 \\
\hline
45 \\
\end{array}
$$

In the tenths column you add **1 + 0 + 2 = 3**. No values to carry over to the ones column on the left of the decimal point.

$$
\begin{array}{r}
1 \\
.095 \\
+\ .250 \\
\hline
.345
\end{array}
$$

The final answer is **.345** or **345** thousandths.

Example: Subtracting 95 thousandths **(.095)** from 25 hundredths **(.25)**.

Step 1: Align the decimal points vertically.

$$
\begin{array}{r}
.25 \\
-\ .095
\end{array}
$$

Step 2: Add zeros as placeholders.

$$
\begin{array}{r}
.250 \\
-\ .095
\end{array}
$$

Step 3: Subtract the columns farthest to the right first and work your way left. Remember to borrow from the next column on the left when the value you are subtracting from is less then the value you are subtracting. In this case, the thousandths column is **0 - 5**. Therefore, you must borrower 1 hundredths (or 10 thousandths) from the hundredths column which will make the thousandths column **10 - 5 = 5**.

$$
\begin{array}{r}
4\ 10 \\
.250 \\
-\ .095 \\
\hline
5
\end{array}
$$

The hundredths column is now **4 - 9**, which also requires you borrow form the tenths column (next column to the left.) 1 tenths is equal to 10 hundredths, which makes the hundredths column **14 - 9 = 5**.

$$
\begin{array}{r}
1\ 14\ 10 \\
.250 \\
-\ .095 \\
\hline
55
\end{array}
$$

In the tenths column you subtract **1 - 0 = 1**. There is no need to borrow from the ones column (next column to the left.)

$$\begin{array}{r} \overset{\scriptsize 1\,14\,10}{.250} \\ -\ \ .095 \\ \hline .155 \end{array}$$

The final answer is **.155** or **155** thousandths.

EXERCISES

Journal Exercise 32: Decimals

Visit the following web sites and work through the problems taking notes in your notebook.

Test your Math Skills:
http://www.kvcc.me.edu/website/frames/websitedata/prospectivestudents/
howtoenroll/pretest_arithmetic.pdf

Take an Accuplacer Review Test:
http://professionals.collegeboard.com/profdownload/accuplacer-sample-questions-
for-students.pdf

_____

_____

_____

_____

_____

_____

_____

_____

Chapter 18

"The average American worker has fifty interruptions a day, of which seventy percent have nothing to do with work." ~ W. Edwards Deming

PERCENTAGES

- Percents represent parts of a whole. Percentage means parts per 100.
- When you say "Percent" you are really saying "per 100." The parts is a number out of 100.

Example 10% = 10 out of 100.
Example 20% = 20 out of 100.

Percent comes from the Latin per centum. The latin word centum means 100. For example a century is 100 years.

A Percentage can also be expressed as a decimal or a fraction.

As a percentage:	**50%**
As a decimal :	**0.5**
As a fraction:	**50/100**

Finding the Percentage

Example: If **8** out of **20** students in a class are boys, what percent of the class is made up of boys?

In this problem, you are being asked "**8** is what percent of **20**?" Since we know that percent is parts per hundred, we can rewrite the fraction.

$$\frac{8}{20} = \frac{x}{100}$$

The question "what percent" tells us that percent is the unknown quantity. This unknown quantity will be represented by **x** in our example above.

In order to solve this problem you must find the equivalent fraction where the whole is 100.

First, you must isolate the x (unknown quantity) on one side of the equation. The great thing about the term equivalent is that it means equal, and as long as you perform the same multiplication or division to both sides of the equation, then the resulting fractions are still equal.

For example, if I isolate the **x** by multiply both sides of the equation above by 100 and then reduce, I can solve for the value of **x** (percent.)

$$100\,\frac{8}{20} = \frac{x}{100}\,100$$

$$\frac{800}{20} = x$$

$$40 = x$$

The final answer is **x = 40.**

Example: Calculate 25% of 80.

In this example, we are given the percentage and are being asked to solve for the equivalent fraction **x/80** where **x** is our unknown quantity. In other words, what number out of **80** is equivalent to **25%**.

We start off by writing the fractions as equivalent fractions, multiplying both sides by **80**, and then reducing. Remember that as long as you perform the same multiplication or division to both sides of the equation, then the resulting fractions are still equal.

$$\frac{25}{100} = \frac{x}{80}$$

$$80\,\frac{25}{100} = \frac{x}{80}\,80$$

$$\frac{2000}{100} = x$$

$$20 = x$$

The final answer is **x = 20.**

Example: **80** is **40%** of what number?

In this example, we are given the percentage and are being asked to solve for the equivalent fraction **80/x** where **x** is our unknown quantity.

We start off by writing the fractions as equivalent fractions. Please note that the **x** is now the denominator.

$$\frac{40}{100} = \frac{80}{x}$$

Remember that as long as you perform the same multiplication or division to both sides of the equation, the resulting fractions are still equal. In this case, you can multiply both sides by **x**. This will help simplify the equation when solving for **x**.

$$x\,\frac{40}{100} = \frac{80}{x}\,x$$

$$x\,\frac{40}{100} = 80$$

Now you can continue to isolate **x** by multiplying both sides by **100, dividing both sides by 40, and then reducing the resulting fraction.**

$$\frac{100}{40} \times \frac{40}{100} = \frac{80}{} \frac{100}{40}$$

$$x = \frac{8000}{40}$$

$$x = \frac{800/4}{4/4} = \frac{200}{1}$$

$$x = 200$$

The final answer is **x = 200.**

Example: Macy's is having a sale. Your favorite pair of shoes are **25%** off the original price. The original price was **$120**. Find the new price.

First we must find the price reduction (how much are you saving.) To find out what **25%** of **$120** is, you must isolate the **x** (unknown value) and then reduce.

$$\frac{25}{100} = \frac{x}{120}$$

$$120 \frac{25}{100} = \frac{x}{120} 120$$

$$\frac{3000}{100} = \frac{30}{1} = x$$

$$30 = x$$

25% of **$120** is **$30**. **$30** is the reduction in price, the savings amount.

To find out what the new price is, you must subtract the reduction (savings) from the original price.

$$\$120 - \$30 = \$90$$

The final answer is **$90.**

EXERCISES

Journal Exercise 33: What number is 80% of 20?

_____

_____

_____

_____

_____

_____

_____

_____

_____

Journal Exercise 34: 3 is what percent of 4?

_____

_____

_____

_____

_____

_____

_____

_____

Journal Exercise 35: 10% of what number is 3?

_____

_____

_____

_____

_____

_____

_____

_____

_____

_____

_____

_____

_____

_____

_____

_____

_____

_____

_____

_____

_____

Chapter 19

"How you think about a problem is more important than the problem itself - So always think positively." ~ Norman Vincent Peale

WORD PROBLEMS

Word or story problems give us a glimpse at how math is used in our day-to-day life. In order to solve a word problem, the problem must be translated into the language of math. When translating a word problem, focus on the facts that are important. Seek out what is essential. Inessential facts can be modified without affecting the meaning of the problem or question.

A variable in an equation is just an unknown quantity. It is often represented by the letter **x**.

Most word problems can be matched to a problem class. A problem class is a common classification of a word or story problem. The letters **a**, **b** and **c** are the known constants or facts.

Problem Classes
- $a + x = b$
- $a * x = b$

- $x = a + b$
- $x = a * b$

As you work through the problem, think of which class the given problem belongs to.

Example: You had $505.00 in your savings account. Your mom gave you some more money. You now have $555.00 in your savings account. How much money did you get from your mom?

> This example fits the problem class $a + x = b$, or $x = b - a$. In this problem **b** is the new savings account balance and **a** is the account balance before your mother gave you the money. In this case, b - a = $555 - $505.
> Therefore x = $555 - $505 = **$50**.

Example: You are a teacher and you have $100 budgeted for notebooks. Each notebook costs $2. How many notebooks can you buy?

> This example fits the problem class $a * x = b$, or $x = b / a$. In this problem **b** is the $100.00 budget and **a** is the cost per book. In this case, b / a = $100/$2.
> Therefore x = $100/$2 = **50** notebooks.

Example: You earned $47,500 in 2008 and $56,200 in 2009. What was your total income for both years?

> This example fits the problem class of $x = a + b$. In this problem x is the total income for both years. In this case, $a + b$ = $47,500 + $56,200.
> Therefore x = $47,500 + $56,200 = **$103,700**.

Example: You enjoy reading fiction books. The book that you are reading has 240 pages. You read 15 pages a day. How many days will it take you to read the entire book?

> This example fits the problem class of $x = a * b$. In this problem x is the number of days it will take you to finish the entire book. In this case, $a * b$ = 240 pages * 1 day/15 pages = 240/15 days = 16 days.

NOTE: The letters **a**, **b** and **c** represent constants or facts. The constants or facts can be whole numbers, fractions, decimals, or percentages.

EXERCISES

Journal Exercise 35: Word Problems

Review: http://www.studygs.net/mathproblems.htm

_____

_____

_____

_____

_____

_____

_____

_____

_____

_____

_____

_____

_____

_____

_____

_____

_____

About the Author

Leticia Colon de Mejias is an accomplished educator and author. Leticia's passion for service through education began during her early teens, when she had the opportunity to walk on fire. Fire walking helped Leticia recognize her self-imposed fears and limitations. This experience opened her world up to the abundance of possibilities. Most of us spend our lives never really facing the things we fear. We mentally push them out of the way. Fire walking helped Leticia empower herself and conquer her fears.

Leticia credits her parents, who were unconventional in their teaching styles, with instilling in her the idea of mind over matter, living in the moment and service to others as a young child. Having been blessed with a "can-do" attitude, Leticia quickly learned that when you believe, anything is possible.

Leticia is a children's book author with several books in print. Her books introduce children to the same concepts she learned as a child. She believes that through reading, we can help children build character, while supporting positive qualities such as humanity, compassion, dedication, integrity, self-awareness and self-esteem. Her book titles can be found at http://www.greatbooks4kids.org.

Leticia is a strong supporter of literacy. She volunteers in the Hartford and Windsor school systems. Along with motivational speaking, Leticia also mentors adult learners and at-risk youth in her native Connecticut.

While working as the educational coordinator for Hartford Hospital, Leticia discovered a common thread among students. She found that students wanted to succeed but were held back by their own fears or lack of knowledge on how to begin, how to set goals and how to follow their dream to fruition. This led her to develop educational programs that have been utilized by schools and businesses alike.

In June 2007, Leticia was awarded the CT Workforce Star Award by Capital Workforce Partners. The award honored her dedication to Hartford adult education and to helping Hartford Hospital employees succeed.

In June 2009, Leticia was awarded the SINA Award by South End Neighbor Alliance. She was presented this prestigious award for her work in the community.

"I love the hospital and value what I do. I feel the programs I am able to support are an extreme benefit to the hospital and the local community. I am grateful to be a part of the hospital's education success and the positive impact it has had on our community." ~ Leticia Colon de Mejias

www.ingramcontent.com/pod-product-compliance
Lightning Source LLC
Chambersburg PA
CBHW081633040426
42449CB00014B/3288